A Gardening Guide to Nature and Health

Beginner's one-stop pocket guide to planning and gardening in 9 easy steps

Katerina Koehlerova

Copyright © 2024 by Katerina Koehlerova

Original Photography by Katerina Koehlerova

Drawn Images by Naomi Kempster

All Rights Reserved

No part of this work may be published, photocopied, stored in a retrieval system, recorded, reproduced, adapted, broadcast, or transmitted in any form or by any means without the prior permission of the copyright owner.

ISBN: 978-1-916626-70-6

To all nature and garden lovers.

Table of Contents

Chapter One: My Gardening Journey 9

Chapter Two: Planning and Design: Size Does Not Matter! 13

Chapter Three: My Gardening Year in Colour and Scent 22

Chapter Four: Growing Fruit for Health 39

Chapter Five: Growing Vegetables for a Healthy Diet 46

Chapter Six: The Herb Garden 54

Chapter Seven: The Wild Flower Garden......................... 62

Chapter Eight: Wildlife in the Garden 69

Chapter Nine: The Water Garden 79

Chapter Ten: Floriography – The Language of Flower 87

Chapter Eleven: Types of Soil 93

Chapter Twelve: In Conclusion 96

Appendix 100

Bibliography 105

Index 107

'The best place to seek God is in a garden. You can dig for him there.'

George Bernard Shaw

Chapter One: My Gardening Journey

Why another book on gardening? There is a wealth of knowledge already available in books, magazines, and the media, all written and presented by people who have unparalleled knowledge: people trained in horticulture and the science behind healthy gardens and healthy growth. This book is different because it is written by a committed amateur, someone who loves gardens and what they give – it is about gardening for the soul rather than perfection. It is about what gives us pleasure, and it is instinctive rather than scientific, experimental rather than perfect. We depend on Mother Nature for the air we breathe, the food we eat, and our mental well-being.

I shall work my way through key ideas and provide you with hints and guidance from my personal experience. Mistakes happen even in the best of gardens, so experiment and persevere until you find your optimum garden ideal. Mental health, the benefits of nature, and protecting the environment are very much topics to consider. Gentle exercise, fresh air, and enjoying the natural world around us all contribute to gardening for well-being and the soul.

The main purpose of this book is to take you on my gardening journey from its beginnings. I work in the IT industry, specifically in sales, but my passion for gardening has encouraged me to share my ideas. Gardening provides an antidote to the pressures of the modern world, emails, and computers: the treadmill of work in artificial environments that can become soul-destroying.

I have been interested in gardening since my childhood in the Czechoslovakian Socialist Republic. My grandparents and family loved the natural world, and my granddad had a bee house. We used to make honey for our friends and commercial purposes. I witnessed my grandmother taking care of plants and flowers in our garden, and she played a significant role in encouraging my interest in gardening. She taught me about plants and how to grow flowers and vegetables, so my passion for gardening is in my genes.

My Parents' House in the Small Town of Plumlov, Czech Republic - Built in 1914

The home of my childhood traces its roots back to 1914. It is set in a pleasing orchard. The pines overlook the grounds of a large, beautiful garden complete with a porch and a slope descending towards an artificial lake. The lush, mixed woods frame and beautify the lake.

The most basic tasks, such as planting and watering, give me inexplicable joy: seeing my healthy garden full of plants, fruit, herbs, and vegetables to pick and eat. I love to bake cakes and cook using the fruit and vegetables I grow. Gardening gives all the benefits of organic and home-grown produce. Nurturing my garden gives me a sense of belonging and brings my soul peace and purpose. It is a source of happiness and inspiration in my life. Why buy expensive products when they can be grown at home?

For me, gardening is like meditation, a perfect way to escape from the chaos of the world. Apart from the benefits of raw and organic products, greenery refreshes your soul. Moreover, the plants we grow have healing properties to keep us healthy and help maintain a balanced life.

I am slowly recovering from a prolonged and painful treatment for oral cancer, and this book has been on my mind all this time. Yes, I do now cherish health more than ever before, and this experience made me even closer to nature and helped me to become one with the healing cycle that gardens offer to us, no matter how small, or large these calm spaces are.

As the world becomes more under threat every day, it is essential to recognise the significance of plants. Plants show humans the path back to nature and teach us how to find our inner balance, a balance between nature and the materialistic world. I have found peace in my life through gardening. Its rewards are immense, keeping us healthy, reducing stress, and adding beauty.

For any tips and tricks and more helpful information, visit my website: www.gardeningnaturehealth.com

Apple Tree Blossoms

Chapter Two: Planning and Design: Size Does Not Matter!

Size does not matter. Whatever the area of your garden, whether it is large, a small, paved patio, a balcony, or even just a window box or sill, now is the time for you to become fully creative and maximise your own growing space. First, measure your growing area. You will have your own ideas, but looking at established gardens can provide inspiration. Some ideas might include low maintenance designs: for example, raised beds or artificial grass; themed or concept areas such as alpine rockeries or herb collections; water features, paving, lighting, hedging, and fencing for boundaries, seating, garden statuary, arches, and ornaments, creating shady areas and attracting wildlife. Plan for colour, texture, and scent and, if possible, add an environmentally important plastic butt for water storage: free standing or fixed to a downpipe. Garden centres sell all shapes and sizes of space-saving and water-saving features.

You might need to consider play areas with extended lawns, bearing in mind all-important safety matters. Do not forget storage and equipment and practical considerations like somewhere to dry your washing. I am lucky enough to have storage space, but there are many budget options on sale. Horizontal lines will make the site seem wider, while vertical lines will give the illusion of greater length. If space is tight, growing vertically allows for underplanting, and pattern and shape can also be achieved by using cordon and espalier fruit trees. You may wish to include a Japanese-style area, or a romantic, formal, or cottage garden. Or maybe you would rather just grow food! Whatever you choose, make the style your own. The choice is yours for the space available. Naturally, your research will include trips to garden centres and gardens of all kinds. Experts are always keen to share their knowledge, and seed catalogues are a vital and valuable source of ideas when planning for the coming seasons. TV programmes, newspaper articles, and the internet are all invaluable sources of knowledge.

When you have mapped out your garden shape on squared paper, you can start to visualise where your features, plants, fruit, and vegetables will fit. Make your mistakes on paper first. It is vitally important to put the right plants in the right space. Work with your growing conditions, and if something doesn't flourish, don't waste energy feeling guilty about the loss: change it. Experience is everything. Sometimes weather conditions take control, and frost, heat, and drought can wreak havoc through no fault of our own. Even the most experienced gardeners have to contend with failures! Remember, gardens evolve with their owners, and mistakes can be corrected. Your taste and needs will inevitably change over time. A cottage garden might be replaced with a more formal design – hard landscaping to grass or vegetable growing but the key to enjoyment is growing the plants you love.

Think about sustaining the environment by reusing plastic pots and seed trays and be creative with containers. Old squash bottles cut in half, seedling pots made from rolled-up newspaper, and empty ice cream pots can all be used for starting seeds and saving money.

Remember that trees are a vital source for soaking up CO_2, and if you only have room for a small ornamental tree in the ground or a pot, the environment will benefit. Offers of cuttings and plants, and seeds from friends or fellow gardeners can provide memories, save money and give pleasure. Personal taste and budget constraints will shape your growing space. Have a look at neighbours' gardens to see what flourishes locally and research the best plants for encouraging butterflies, birds, and the all-important bees for pollination.

The photographs below are of my garden, which has evolved over many years and may give you some ideas which you can incorporate into your own growing areas.

My Evolving Garden with a Small Water Feature - Mermaid Fountain

The patio area was extended, and the adjacent flowerbeds were enlarged. An ornamental cherry provides shade and privacy as well as breaking up the sight line along the fence.

Pots were introduced to provide seasonal colour and extend planting areas. The soil along the left-hand side was inadequate for growing even small trees as it was full of brick rubble to quite a depth. However, the buddleia [the butterfly bush] provides nectar for butterflies and bees. It can grow in nearly any soil and provides shade over the bench next to the pond.

The water feature contains a mermaid fountain that was made locally, and the sound of running water is relaxing and soothing.

Yellow Water Irises

Water lilies, irises, and marsh marigolds thrive in the four-foot-deep pond, which attracts frogs and diverse pond life. The pots contain an olive tree, oleander, peach tree, Callistemon [bottle brush], lemon tree, and an azalea - all of which provide fruit or seasonal colour. Herbs in pots surround the pond: mint, chives, basil, thyme, sage, parsley, and rosemary. They all have the added benefits of producing scent as you brush past, as well as giving fresh ingredients for cooking. You can create a diverse and instant garden to any scale by using pots and containers for flowers, shrubs, fruit, and vegetables with the extra advantage that they can be moved to create different combinations and designs.

The heron in the corner was bought from neighbours who were leaving the area and downsizing.

Heron Sculpture - Garden Ornament

Garden ornaments can be bought from salvage firms and at auction, helping to add an extra dimension to the surrounding greenery. At one time, lavender lined the left-hand dividing wall, but it did not flourish in the shade, so it was replanted successfully in the sunny areas. I replaced the lavender with red camellias and red roses, which give spring and summer colour. To the right can be seen a heuchera [Sugar Plum] in an antique pot bought locally at auction.

Heuchera - Sugar Plum in an Antique Cream Glazed Pottery Flowerpot

The colour of the plant and pot are complementary and give all year-round interest.

Either side of the stable back door can be seen as a trough for annual planting and variegated evergreen euonymus. Above is an ornamental cherub planter containing succulents. The French doors are framed with a climbing red rose which gives scent in the summer, and rosehips for the birds and colour in the winter. Below, the green man stands guard (glazed terracotta figurine), signifying rebirth, representing the cycle of new growth each spring, or of course, you could source a much rarer green woman.

A social space is important for me, and a table and seating in a sunny area on the patio with an umbrella for shade and a space for quiet reading is one of the features I enjoy. The garden can also provide extra room for cooking on the barbecue and spending time with friends and family.

The dividing walls deliberately set apart the grass area on either side of the path. This is part of the low-maintenance plan. The two magnolia trees mark the division: Magnolia Stellata gives spring scent and colour, while the other, Magnolia Grandiflora, displays flamboyant tea-plate white flowers in the summer.

Magnolia Grandiflora

The bottom area of the garden has space for growing fruit and summer vegetables in containers and harvesting fresh produce is satisfying and exciting and makes it all worthwhile. Even a humble window box can be used for herbs or leaves.

Gardening, however large or small, is therapeutic, health-giving, and good for the well-being of the environment and us. Size doesn't matter!

Rhododendron Gomer Waterer flowering end of May or in June

Chapter Three: My Gardening Year in Colour and Scent

One of the delights of any garden is the combination of colour and scent, giving visual and olfactory pleasure. They are highly restorative so include fragrant flowers in your garden plan. It is impossible to add every plant, and your unique taste will play a part. I have chosen just a few of the favourites in my garden to give you some ideas and some hints as the year unfolds. Use colour as a canvas. Planting cool colours at the bottom of the garden adds depth and gives the illusion of space, lightening, and brightening shady areas, while hot colours are better closer.

Phlox in the Bloom

In the main, I am using common names rather than the Latin derivations, but if you want to learn the generic terms, gardening books will give you all the information you need.

The garden in January can still have colour and scent from the brilliant white bark of the paper birch to the fragrant witch hazel, which has scented flowers on bare branches.

Delicate snowdrops are some of the first flowers to herald the spring along with winter aconites. The Cornus or dogwoods, with their brightly coloured stems in reds, oranges, and yellows, brighten dull days and the winter garden. Some bamboos also have colourful stems adding to the winter palette.

My favourite is the Golden Bamboo which sits next to and compliments the variegated leaf and bright red berries of Golden King holly. Bamboos add another sensory layer as the wind rustles through their evergreen leaves. Christmas roses produce white flowers from winter to early spring, and the winter Iris [Iris unguicularis] is an evergreen border plant with large blue flowers which create an unexpected flash of colour on grey days. Now is the time to think about ordering seeds for summer plants, cleaning pots and seed trays, and checking that the pond is free from ice, and if you have pansies in winter pots, keep deadheading, and the flowers will keep coming.

Frost on Evergreen Shrubs

February is still cold, but the garden has much to enjoy. Cyclamen, a low clump-forming perennial with bright flowers and marbled leaves; the bright leaves of the Euonymous Silver Queen and winter heathers make the colourful ground cover. Crocus bulbs, yellow, white, and purple, will begin to appear, and camellias with their peony-like flowers start to open their buds but can be damaged by frost. Later, bulbs start to show their leaves above ground and, because of global warming and its inevitable climate changes, can flower early. It is important to check plants that need staking and to continue to clear the beds of winter debris.

March has variable weather, but the garden is waking up. Plants emerging include the blue grape hyacinth and daffodils, and narcissus. The pussy willow [Salix caprea] develops its tactile buds, and hazel trees form their yellow catkins announcing warmer days.

Forsythia, with its deep yellow flowers, is a stand-alone shrub but can also be used as hedging, and I like to pick the bare branches and bring them inside, where they will soon burst into flower. The flowering quince or the Japanese quince [Chaenomeles japonica] produces beautiful pink or scarlet flowers, with the added advantage of yellow fruit in the autumn, which can be used for pickles and jam. Primroses pop up and will naturalise by spreading their seed, giving pleasure year after year. Hardy annuals can be sown now for summer colour, and it is a good time to divide perennials to share with friends. Snowdrops will benefit from being divided while their stems are still green and start deadheading early flowering daffodils, so they don't set seed and will come back stronger next year.

Daffodils 'February Gold'

Scented plants begin to appear in the warmer days of April: hyacinths, lily of the valley, viburnums, and jasmine perfume the air. The blossoms of cherry, apple, and almond trees in pinks and whites hang in clusters, some ornamental and some preparing for the fruit they will bear later in the year. The unusual flower heads of the snakes-head fritillary, clematis, and star-shaped flowers of the Magnolia Stellata all make their appearance. Plants that give pleasure over several seasons, like the prickly berberis shrub, Berberis darwinii, are certainly useful, and in April, they have bright orange flowers, which develop into blue-black berries in the autumn. The promise of summer and longer days is an encouragement to get out and get busy. This is a good month to start preparing pots and hanging baskets, but there is still the threat of frost, so if you are tempted to get ahead, then keep the containers in a frost-free environment. Check your seed packets for the best method and optimum time to sow your own plants.

A lot of gardeners feel that May is the best month in the garden. The days are increasingly warmer, and some spring bulbs are still in flower, especially tulips and scented hyacinths. The bees and birds are busy, and the deciduous trees are in leaf. Spectacular rhododendrons come into their own – if your garden isn't large enough, then there are wonderful displays in public gardens which embrace every colour, from white to peach and from gold to red. It is always a pleasure to explore the wider environment. Delicate clematis, bluebells, wisteria, scented lilac, and purple allium with their lollipop-shaped flowers all burst into bloom, and the golden yellow marsh marigolds brighten the ponds and water features.

Clematis 'The Duchess of Cornwall'

Creating colour schemes and patterns with pots can go ahead now. If you don't have the space to grow your own, then the garden centres have ready-planted arrangements, but it is fun to create your very own displays, and there are so many options. Stick to your budget – plant buying is compulsive, and there are so many lovely bedding plants on offer! Often bargains can be found from fellow gardeners who grow their own and always grow too many. It is fun to exchange and share, and one packet of seeds can make many seedlings. Edges can be softened with trailing plants like ivy, and adding height can give an extra perspective. The trough by my back door is the perfect place for bright petunias, which are easily cared for, and fuchsias offer great value for money and flower until the first frosts. Geraniums don't require much watering, and cuttings from favourites are very successful and easy to grow. Baskets and pots dry out quickly, so remember to water them daily; they do benefit from weekly feeds. Watch the weather forecast to ensure there is no frost before letting the summer colour run wild.

One of my favourite plants to sow now is cosmos, and they can be grown so easily in seed trays at home. They give endless colour through the late summer if they are regularly deadheaded, but they do need staking as they can grow tall. White Purity and bright pink Dazzle look amazing planted among the perennials, and lots can be propagated from one packet of seed.

June is a wonderful month in the garden. The pots and containers come into their own now, and there are so many opportunities for colour and scent. Honeysuckle smells wonderful in the early evening and can be trained to soften fences and walls. Large flowering clematis can be trained through trees, as can rambling roses. I have had success growing a rose through the lower branches of an apple tree, and the perennial geraniums look amazing at the front of flower beds with their pink, blue and purple flowers.

Lavender Border in a Flower Bed

Lavender begins to flower, and later in the year, the fragrant lavender heads can be picked and dried for lavender bags to scent drawers and cupboards. It is therapeutic to take some time just to sit and enjoy what you have created.

Buddleia 'Black Knight' Butterfly Bush

July is one of the warmest months and the month for roses: climbing roses, shrub roses, rambling roses, and bush roses. It would be hard to choose a favourite out of these lovely traditional flowers, and their size and the size of your growing space will dictate how many, and which type you choose. I have some in a pot on the patio, but they can be trained up a wall or grace a flowerbed and will provide colour, scent, and structure – the choice is yours. Deadheading keeps them flowering, and a vase of home-grown roses is a delight and brings the outside in. Nasturtiums, nigella, and poppies are all in flower and are easy to grow from seed. Sowing sweet peas earlier in the year is easy, but young plants can be bought quite cheaply from garden centres. Their scented and colourful blooms proliferate in July, and as long as they are picked regularly and are not left to go to seed, they thrive and produce their multi-coloured blooms for weeks. Making wigwams from garden canes gives them support, and they make a lovely addition to the summer garden. Everywhere is full of colour, and the bees are busy. Unfortunately, so are the pests!

Snail feeding on leaves of a shrub

I try to be an organic gardener and shy away from chemical controls. The consensus is that healthy plants are less likely to be attacked by pests and diseases, so keep watering and feeding, and if you want to use controls, that is your choice. A good way to remove greenflies and blackflies is to rub them off with the fingers, which may or may not appeal, but it works. Ladybird Beetles eat aphids, frogs, and birds eat insects and slugs, and some advocate going out in the garden at night with a torch to collect slugs and snails. If it is particularly wet, the slugs can play havoc with osta plants, but I still prefer to leave the snails for the blackbirds, and if I lose a few plants, then that is part of my gardening journey. Nematodes are a natural aid for removing slugs and are easily sourced and applied.

Bee pollinating Dahlia

August, and already we are in the eighth month of the year and moving towards the end of full summer. Watering is important as the dry and warm days take their toll, and the birds need water too. Buddleia is in full bloom attracting the butterflies and bees, and I love perpetual flowering begonias in pots to brighten the patio. Hydrangeas and echinacea, late-flowering clematis, white marguerites, fuchsias, and penstemons all compete, and the pots and hanging baskets continue to flourish. Deadheading is important to prolong the flowering life of some species, and it is a good month to trim hedges as the birds have fledged. There are opportunities to collect seeds from some plants; shaking the poppy heads into a container will release the seeds, leaving the ornamental seed heads in the beds where they give added architectural interest. It is a good time to choose bulbs for the spring and decide what you might want to change and grow in the coming year. The evenings are still warm, and eating and cooking outside is the perfect way to enjoy the last days and summer evenings before autumn kicks in.

In September, some autumn colours begin to appear. There is a sense that the garden will soon be changing, and thoughts inevitably turn to the colder months. However, a large clump of yellow rudbeckia and perennial sunflowers give welcome bursts of colour. The echinacea seed heads are tactile, and with luck, their seeds will fall and set new plants. The seed heads provide ornamental interest and a habitat for insects, and food for birds. Ornamental grasses are a good source of colour, with lots of shades of green and interesting feathery textures. The dahlias are still blooming and will flower into the autumn if regularly deadheaded. They have colour for every scheme – hot or cool. Now is the time to plant spring flowering bulbs, and hyacinths can be forced to give colour and scent, to give as Christmas gifts, or to enjoy on a window sill when the flower garden is becoming dormant.

I am not a winter person, but in October, the autumn colours give the illusion of warmth as the temperatures drop and the days shorten. All the maple varieties turn into fire colours of red, orange, and yellow, and apples are ready for harvesting, all of which make up for the lack of flowers. There are rose hips, the autumn crocus, and seed heads for interest, and it is a good time to look at catalogues for tulip bulbs to plant now. Michaelmas daisies which came from my mother's garden are now flowering in mine. Winter pansies in pots can add splashes of colour – pop the pots in the flower beds or where they can be seen through the windows on gloomy days. Raking leaves for mulch and compost and clearing the spent perennials is good exercise and the October Garden is a good time for reflection and planning. Delicate plants might need protection now – for example, my lemon tree. Autumn is a good time to plant new trees as the roots will establish and benefit from the winter rain.

Parthenocissus quinquefolia known as 'Virginia Creeper'

The garden centres have lovely displays of inexpensive chrysanthemums in November, which are tempting, and I have kept them for several years. This is the month when plants with berries come into their own – bright holly, pyracantha, viburnum, and rose hips all provide colour and food for the birds. Evergreen plants give colour in different shades of green, and there may not be the variety of the summer palette, but there is still a great deal to admire. Birds and squirrels are entertaining visitors and hanging feeders on bare branches is well worth the cost. Wrap up warm and explore the beds.

Viburnum tinus 'French White' flowering from December to April

December – the Christmas month – and the garden centres sell lots of plants that are meant as gifts but the odd treat to brighten the window sills is tempting. Winter jasmine is a welcome sight, mine helping to disguise a shed, and there is always some to pick for the Christmas table arrangement. I appreciate the holly bushes in the dark, cold days with their bright berries, and if you hunt, there are signs of regeneration. Checking over the garden tools is a good plan, too, so they are ready for the new growing year.

Holly 'Green Alaska' (Ilex) with Glossy Green Leaves

With the promise of a new gardening year, it is time to reflect on what has worked in the garden and what hasn't - whether a new flower bed might work in the design, or some new hedging, or maybe whether there is room for a fruit tree. Every experience is a learning experience, and sometimes serendipitous accidents hold the clue. Make your memories, learn from your mishaps, enjoy your successes, and have fun!

Raspberry Bush offering its Late Summer Fruit

Chapter Four: Growing Fruit for Health

Picking fruit from your own plants, bushes, and trees is a sensory pleasure, as well as providing delicious food for cooking. Your chance of success is greatly enhanced if you buy plants that are certified free from pests, diseases, or viruses. Soft fruits like strawberries, blueberries, raspberries, gooseberries, and blackberries all yield large amounts of fruit and provide a variety of shapes, textures, and colours in your garden.

The quintessential summer strawberries can be grown in hanging baskets and all sorts of containers. They can also provide ground cover. This fruit can help protect your heart, provide good cholesterol, and lower your blood pressure.

Packed with vitamins, fibre, and particularly high levels of antioxidants known as polyphenols, strawberries are a delicious sodium-free, fat-free, cholesterol-free, low-calorie food.

Blueberries, often described as a superfood, are sweet, nutritious, and hugely popular. They are low in calories and very high in nutrients and antioxidants, which may help prevent unstable cell-damaging molecules from attacking your body. They also claim to slow ageing and reduce the risk of heart disease. Their dark blue-black colour makes them an attractive choice for desserts, cooked or raw, and they are deliciously scattered on cereals or used as a snack.

Like most dessert fruits, raspberries, grown from canes, benefit from full sun, which helps ripening and pollination. They are also full of vitamins, minerals, antioxidants, and fibre. They come in four different colours: red, black, purple, and gold. Red raspberries are the most common, and fresh raspberries can be harvested from June to October. They make lovely jams or can be eaten as a treat just as they are. The birds love them, and if you would rather not share, they can be protected with fruit cages.

Gooseberries are commonly used in fruit desserts, preserves, or served in cooked sauces for meat. They are also low in calories, fat-and cholesterol-free, and a good source of essential nutrients, including vitamin C, vitamin A, manganese, and dietary fibre. They are delicious and easy-to-grow soft fruit with a range of varieties for eating or cooking. They prefer the sun and can be trained as cordons to save space or planted in containers, making them ideal for smaller gardens. Gooseberry plants need little attention apart from pruning, watering in dry spells, and feeding in spring to boost harvests.

Blackberries, often a wild fruit seen growing in woodland and hedgerows, are full of vitamins C and K, high in fibre, and high in manganese. There are claims that brain functioning is enhanced by including them in your diet. They come from brambles, which are a type of thorny bush that can spread if not controlled. They freeze well, so they can be used for winter desserts when you can unlock the summer that has just passed. According to folk legend, the Devil stamps on blackberries at Michaelmas on September 29th, and the fruit should not be gathered after that day. It is also said that the Devil spits on them on October 10th. These old tales point out that the fruit should be picked by these dates as they begin to deteriorate as the days get cooler. If there is no room for blackberries in your garden, then they can be gathered for free in hedgerows and make a fun foraging trip out. Sloe berries from the blackthorn trees [Prunus spinosa] are another fruit that can be gathered in the countryside and can be used to make delicious gin for gifts at Christmas.

Other soft fruits you may wish to consider are blackcurrants and redcurrants. They are also high in antioxidants to boost the immune system. They will help your body to fight infection and viruses more easily. They are easy to grow, producing jewel-like bunches of berries in mid-summer. Their sharp flavour makes them suitable for use in pies and jams, and cordials, like cassis from blackcurrants, which is delicious mixed with white wine for a Kir cocktail to drink outside on a summer's evening.

Apples, pears, cherries, and plums are relatively easy to grow. Growing as espaliers or cordons saves space and gives vertical interest. Fruit trees vary enormously in height, so make sure you check the tree's likely size. If using containers, terracotta pots are preferable as

Pear Tree in Summer

they give greater protection from frost, and all trees will benefit from mulches of well-rotted compost and regular feeding and watering.

Perhaps apples are the most popular and versatile fruit of all. There are reported to be 7,000 varieties worldwide, so the choice is huge. They are a common ingredient for pies, crumbles, cookies, muffins, jam, a sauce to accompany pork, and delicious eaten raw. They are a very healthy fruit whose benefits, such as the provision of antioxidants like vitamin E, a source of fibre, and polyphenols, have been widely researched. They may help to lower cholesterol and aid bone health. Whether your garden is large or has limited space, there is usually room to grow at least one apple variety. Self-pollinators mean that a single tree can still provide an ample crop of fruit. Apples ripen at different times, so they can be picked over a period of weeks. They can be carefully stored in a dry, cool place or frozen for use later in the year. If you feel adventurous, you could have a go at making cider or apple juice.

Bramley Apple Harvest in August

Plums are full of fibre. They can also boost your body's production of adiponectin, a hormone that helps regulate your blood sugar levels. Prunes (dried plums) may help reduce bone loss and may even reverse it. Their history is interesting. Some claim that they first grew in China thousands of years ago, then made their way to Japan, parts of Europe, and America. Others claim that most plums evolved from the sloe or blackthorn and were well-known in ancient Egypt. They have been found in tombs in Thebes to provide food for the afterlife, while the Romans admired them for their laxative effects. The delicious eating variety, the Victoria plum, was probably named for Queen Victoria at her 1837 coronation. Today, more than 2,000 varieties grow all over the world. Plums add sweetness to salads and desserts, can be bottled or frozen, and make good jam. Be careful when picking, as sometimes the wasps get there first!

Rhubarb, a once popular fruit, should not be forgotten. It is an attractive, hardy perennial with large leaves and pink, red, or greenish leaf stalks. This delicious fruit can be used as a dessert in pies, fools, and crumbles. The flavour of rhubarb varies in sweetness depending on the age of the stems but don't eat the leaves as they can be poisonous. Rhubarb is extremely easy to grow, and plants crop well for many years. Rhubarb is rich in antioxidants, and, as with so many of these fruits, it may help protect you from many health-related issues such as heart disease, cancer, and diabetes.

Growing fruit is satisfying, nourishing, and aesthetically pleasing. It is a welcome addition to any garden, although space can be an issue. However, a few strawberries in a pot or a small fruit tree in a container can still give homegrown pleasure. Many fruit growing farms offer the opportunity to 'pick your own', a satisfying activity for the family and an encouragement for children to sample a new flavour as they harvest. If your growing area is limited, other people's spaces can be used as an extension of your garden. Fresh air, exercise, and nourishment all combine to promote health and well-being.

Bush Tomatoes

Chapter Five: Growing Vegetables for a Healthy Diet

Along with its gardening ideas, this book focuses on well-being and mindfulness, and vegetable gardening can be transformative in so many ways. We are told that we are what we eat, and picking some healthy home-grown vegetables is an incentive to improve our diet for the better. We know that 'five a day' is the recommended dietary requirement, and research has shown that eating less meat is good for the environment as well as for ourselves. With changing attitudes to meat eating, veganism and vegetarianism are on the rise, and growing one's own not only helps improve our health for the better but encourages fresh air and exercise. The vitamins and minerals found in vegetables help us to fight disease, and a good mixture in the daily diet can only be beneficial. Another important consideration is that growing our own does save air miles.

Growing vegetables depends on the space one has, but they can be grown very successfully in containers, even in flower borders, where things like decorative runner beans in wigwam structures can be grown at the back of the beds to provide both colour and food. Gaps in the herbaceous borders can be used for the colourful Swiss chard with its orange and yellow stems, low in calories but high in vitamins and minerals, or the red-leaved lettuces for summer salads. Peppers, chillies, and aubergines look colourful and attractive and show that edible plants can be as aesthetically pleasing as many flowers. Cottage gardens have always been used for this kind of planting, so choose what you would like to grow, let your imagination run wild, and experiment.

If a cottage garden look isn't a viable option, I have a trough, bought from a garden centre, which sits on a patio area and which has a surprising amount of space for different vegetables. Raised beds are another useful growing method, especially for sore backs, as they obviate the need for excessive bending. Those lucky enough to have a large vegetable garden or allotment can be more adventurous and almost self-sufficient, but for most of us, the clever use of pots can be used to grow all manner of delicious and health-giving extras. Arrangements of pots on durable shelving can make an attractive and space-saving display, and balconies and window boxes can, with ingenuity, provide the space for a satisfying harvest. The larger the container, the better the harvest, plus they have the added advantage that they won't dry out so quickly. Commercially bought grow bags can be used for just about any vegetable and can increase the growing space, especially on a balcony or a patio.

What one grows is a personal choice and depends on what you enjoy eating or regularly buy, but salad crops, tomatoes, cucumbers, beetroot, radishes, chillies, and onions are favourites of mine. Maybe try some of the more unusual vegetables, like squashes, pak choi, or celeriac, but whatever you choose, don't be disheartened if the pests get there first or the weather doesn't cooperate. As experience constantly shows us, every gardener has to deal with failures and frustrations! Birds, slugs, snails, and aphids all want to share, and the climate, especially in relation to climate change, can take its toll with unseasonable weather, drought, winds, and excessive heat. Despite the challenges, whether growing from seeds or buying and swapping plants, vegetable growing is an exciting part of gardening with healthy rewards. They are full of vitamins and minerals and are an indispensable part of our nutrition. In the kitchen, gluts can be frozen, preserved, and used in the barren months for a taste of summer and, in the happy event of a large harvest, can be used for nourishing soups in the colder weather. Remember that vegetables love sunshine and good, rich, organic soil, so choose your compost carefully and pick a sunspot for your pots or the vegetable bed. Some will need staking, and regular watering is essential, especially in periods of drought. As with all plants, the use of liquid fertilisers increases success rates.

Spring is a good time to start cutting and come again salad leaves, and they can be grown successfully from seed and, if protected from frost, can provide food throughout the year. They can be started in a greenhouse or on a sunny window sill and give rapid results. Using succession planting and intercropping will provide nourishment throughout the growing season for continuous crops of healthy salads.

Freshly picked sweet tomatoes are always delicious and full of goodness. They can be planted in containers, commercially bought grow bags, or directly into the ground, or the tumbling varieties look decorative in hanging baskets. There are lots of tomatoes to choose from. You might favour the large beefsteak variety or the small cherry tomatoes, which ripen more quickly and are not labour-intensive. Read the instructions on the seed packets or plant labels for the optimum growing tips. If you are lucky enough to have a greenhouse, tomatoes benefit from the warmth and protection. Remember that tomatoes need sunshine to boost their sweetness, so aim for a sunny spot. Once the fruits begin to set, they do like a regular application of a tomato fertiliser and careful watering – too much and the skins can split. At the end of the growing season, any unripened fruits can be left on a sunny window sill, but they can also be used to make tasty green tomato chutney.

Cucumbers are perfect for a large container, and climbing up wigwam supports, they are an attractive addition to vegetable growing areas. Picked, prepared, and added to salad, they are well worth a try. Radishes, spring onions, and herbs can be used to intercrop between the taller vegetables, and summer salads can be on the plate within minutes of harvesting. No shop-bought vegetable can taste anywhere near as delicious or provide so much satisfaction.

Potatoes are a versatile vegetable, a source of carbohydrates and vitamin C, and are great fun to grow. Children love to dig and see how many they can find from one seed potato, and it is a good introduction for them to growing their own. Because of the amount of space they use, a good way of experimenting with this crop is to use sacks. Any sort of heavy-duty plastic sack can work, and it is a good way of reusing compost bags. Put about three seed potatoes in some compost and as they grow, keep adding more compost until the tops die off and they are ready to harvest. They will need watering and maybe some liquid feed but a delicious source of food for little effort. Eating one's own new potatoes, garnished with butter and mint from the herb garden, or baked in their skins, makes any effort worthwhile - and everyone loves a chip!

Spinach is one of the most accepted healthy vegetables, easy to grow, and high in Vitamin A, iron, and antioxidants. It can be eaten raw in salads or takes only seconds to cook. Spinach enhances curries and pasta dishes, and the perpetual variety replenishes itself with little effort from us. Carrots, cooked or crunchily raw, are another source of Vitamin A and are thought to maintain good eyesight. Broccoli is a good source of Vitamin C and Vitamin K, and flavoursome garlic has long been acknowledged as an aid to good heart health and circulation. It is often referred to as nature's antibiotic.

Sprouts maybe not be the most favoured green vegetables but are full of vitamins and minerals and are high in potassium. They are surprisingly good raw, shredded in a homemade coleslaw, or cooked with bacon and chestnuts.

Peas and beans are a natural source of fibre and protein and a satisfying crop if you have the space. French beans can be grown without staking and picked young and often are delicious. Without exception, all vegetables are high in antioxidants and contribute to our well-being.

Children are often resistant to eating vegetables but encouraging them to be involved in planting and picking the fruits of their labour can be game-changing. Even something as simple as a pot of cress on the window sill, maybe grown in the shape of the initial letter of their name or as 'hair' in half of a decorated eggshell, can be the start of a love of growing. There is hardly any waiting time before the seeds germinate, an added plus for impatient small growers.

As with all gardening, personal taste is everything, so consider what you like to eat. If one facet of the vegetable garden becomes a chore and gives no pleasure or satisfaction, then try something different. It is worth persevering and maintaining interest by trying something new, trying something less, ignoring the unsuccessful, and building on the victories. Growing vegetables can be very therapeutic, feeding the body, mind, and senses. There is nothing quite like the pleasure of adding fresh produce to a dish of delicious food with the knowledge that it has come from your own kitchen garden: the crunch of a freshly picked carrot or radish, the sweetness of a tomato, or the first new potatoes, organically grown and picked by you, from garden to pot to plate.

Finally, try to plan vegetables in rainbow colours as part of your meals. They will look colourful and appetising and will be a reminder that the rainbow is the spiritual symbol of hope.

Pumpkin Harvest in September- October

Calendula Also Known as Marigold

Chapter Six: The Herb Garden

The growing of herbs has a long history, and science has revealed that old wives' tales about the medicinal properties of plants and herbs often have a basis in fact. Accusations of 'quackery', sorcery and witchcraft meant that in the past, traditional practitioners of herbal solutions needed to be circumspect. They handed down their recipes and 'cures' through the generations, often at risk of persecution after false claims from disgruntled neighbours. Now, as with many things, scientific research plays a part. Commercial herbs and supplements are big business and are easily and legitimately bought from supermarkets and health food shops. However, a herb garden or herbs in a flowerpot help to stimulate our senses in a way far removed from the laboratories of commercial companies.

Herbs can do far more for you than just a garnish, and the use of herbs to promote health and well-being can be traced back to ancient times. They have been cultivated throughout history. Hippocrates (c.460-370 B.C.) listed over 400 medicinal herbs, and Aristotle (c.272-287 B.C.) contributed further research. Nicolas Culpeper (1616 – 1654), a botanist, herbalist, physician, and astrologer, published his *Complete Herbal* in the 17th century, which was described as a comprehensive dictionary of nearly all herbs, in the hope that ordinary people would find it an accessible way to explore solutions to better health. He didn't necessarily practise what he preached! His own life was full of vices – he drank, smoked, and was reportedly funny and rude. It was a time when medical practices were unregulated, and the book was an instant success and remains in print today.

If you want to explore growing herbs and increase your herbal knowledge, The Chelsea Physic Garden by the Thames in London is a beautiful space and is well worth a visit. It is one of the oldest botanical gardens in Europe, and it began its life in 1673, supported by the Worshipful Company of Apothecaries. Within its four-acre site, there is a section on the use of herbs for medicine. As well as many different kinds of plants and trees, there is an abundance of herbs with explanations for their culinary and medical use and how to grow them. There are plants to buy and experts to ask, as well as an opportunity for a delicious lunch, all contributing to a fascinating day out close to the centre of London.

History apart, the purpose of this chapter is about herbs for fragrance, aroma, and flavour, and it is **not** intended for medicinal purposes. It is important to remember they are not a substitute for prescribed medication and always seek advice from reliable herbalists or medical practitioners if you want to follow this route, as some herbs can cause adverse reactions.

Salvia 'Caradonna

As elsewhere in the garden, it is important to recognise plants with toxic properties. For example, foxgloves, opium poppies, lily of the valley, and cowslips should never be confused with edible herbs. Fragrance does not mean that all plants can be eaten safely.

Herbs are lovely plants, adaptable and easy to grow either from seed or as young plants from garden centres. When choosing a place for your herbs, the best position for culinary use is as near to the kitchen as possible so the leaves can be picked easily. Whether in a pot on the window ledge or a more formal herb garden, most herbs love the sunshine, albeit some will thrive in the shade. Planting in pots, containers, and window boxes is an excellent and convenient way to grow herbs, but they will need regular watering and good light. If you are planting your herbs in the soil, loam-based is probably best, but if your soil is heavy clay, then pots may be preferable. When planting mint, a good hint is to put the roots in a pot which can then be plunged into the ground – Mint is a thug and can soon take over the herb space. Herbal borders can look very attractive, and you can create an impressive display by breaking a bed up into squares and circles.

A useful tip is to buy growing herbs from the supermarket, which can be separated into different seedlings to get more plants for your money. Basil works well potted up like this and smells delicious on a window sill, ready to add instant Mediterranean freshness to recipes.

When harvesting, new growth is encouraged by regular picking as it strengthens the development of the plant. Most herbs reach their best flavour just before they flower, and to prevent the plant from becoming woody or spindly, select the young leaves before they become tough and pick them regularly to maintain the new growth. The younger the leaves, the better the flavour. Perennial herbs will produce several pickings each year and will benefit from being sheared to encourage new leaves.

Tied in bunches and hanging in an airy place for use when the season is over, good herbs to dry are bay leaves, thyme, and rosemary as they hold their flavour and aroma for about a year, but there is no comparison with freshly picked leaves. Dried herbs do tend to be stronger than fresh herbs, so larger amounts of fresh herbs are needed in recipes. Fresh herbs can transform a dish by adding depth to the flavour as well as adding brightness and interest. Fresh herbs, like mint and parsley, chopped small, can be frozen in a little water in ice cube trays which are easy to add to recipes. There is nothing nicer than lavender bags made with dried lavender flowers to scent drawers and cupboards and to give as gifts for friends. Fresh sprigs of lavender added to a bath can help relax and ease muscles and encourage rest and mindfulness after a hard day in the garden.

Some are very attractive, and including herbs in a bouquet of freshly picked garden flowers adds fragrance to a room.

Roman Chamomile

Herbs are a major resource for cooking both in the kitchen and outside, and freshly picked herbs on the barbecue can add another sensory level to alfresco entertainment. The air will be scented, and appetites will be stimulated. Your cooking preferences will determine which herbs you grow and learning about how fresh herbs enhance various dishes can be exciting and add to the pleasure of cooking.

Some of my favourites are garlic for just about anything, basil for pesto and pasta, rosemary with its pretty pale blue flowers for lamb, chives for potato salad, mint for new potatoes, mint sauce and mint tea, parsley, and fennel for fish, sage, and thyme for stuffing and adding flavour to sauces – the possibilities are endless. The bright orange flowers of nasturtiums not only brighten the herb garden, but their peppery taste is a lovely addition to salads.

When choosing the best positions for plants, herbs that will grow in clay soils are angelica, chives, comfrey, fennel, lemon balm [Melissa officinalis], and peppermint. Those that thrive in dry conditions are the Mediterranean flavours of bay laurel, garlic, lavender, oregano, rosemary, sage, and thyme. If you have a lot of shade, then try container growing so the pots can be moved to find optimum lighting. Basil, chives, parsley, thyme, oregano, and sage are perhaps the most common everyday herbs, but why not experiment with tarragon, horseradish, or sweet cicely?

Herbs not only enhance our taste buds but have an aesthetic appeal. Powerful and reminiscent emotions can be aroused by the memory of a particular scent. The touch of different textures, like the feathery fennel, and the pleasure of releasing the fragrance when brushing past overhanging herbs all add to the pleasure of this aspect of the garden. A chamomile lawn and thyme planted between stepping stones can add an extra sensory level, and it is an acknowledged fact that people with disabilities, mental health difficulties, or sensory impairment can benefit from the scents of a calming herbal garden.

Chapter Seven: The Wild Flower Garden

It sounds contradictory to deliberately grow a wildflower garden when gardening seems to be all about designing, planning, and controlling the growth of plants, flowers, bushes, and trees. After all, we, as a species, evolved to become agriculturalists and cultivators when we settled on the land and wrestled with it to give us food to survive. The enemy was weeds and non-cultivated species. But now that we appear to dominate our environment, the idea of having a part of the garden that is governed by less rigid arrangements seems desirable.

But what is meant by a wildflower garden? What benefits can it give us? We can try to answer these questions by starting with the sheer pleasure we experience when we come across a wildflower meadow when we turn the corner of a pathway in the country and suddenly see masses of flowers waving majestically. In the meadow, mother nature is the landscaper.

Painters like Renoir popularised images of poppies surrounded by a myriad of blue, yellow, and purple flowers spread like a palette before us. Beauty or aesthetics develop as we age, and more and more experiences provide us with choices from which we form our tastes and our artistic standards. Everyone develops an aesthetic sense, and scenes of natural beauty are high on our list of desirable experiences.

Several needs converge in our appreciation of wildflowers, which generally satisfy those aesthetic needs. It is a similar need to the country garden look that is so charming, colourful, and visually stunning. But the wildflower garden is artful. It is somewhat paradoxical: it is not created by emptying packets of wildflower seeds over an empty patch and waiting for the end result. Like many people, I have tried and failed to create a wildflower garden. So, what did I learn from my failure?

I learned that I was being lazy! I expected ordinary soil in which I grew cultivated plants to spring into action with wildflower seeds. The empty patch looked right. It was uncared for and scruffy looking. Time would be my architect. It would be spectacular!

Unfortunately, my ambition outstripped my skills. Nothing happened. The patch did, however, grow invasive weeds of all sorts. Back to the garden planner and several books on the subject later, I realised how arrogant I had been. It was not the worst kind of hubris, and Zeus did not send a thunderbolt, but the weeds were sufficient rebuke. I longed for lack of structure, colour, and scent. If only I could follow the yellow brick road to reach wildflower nirvana. I had read that such gardens produce food for us and animals as well as being medicinal. They are especially attractive and indeed essential to bees, butterflies, birds, and all sorts of wildlife, as well as reducing greenhouse gasses.

Most species of wildflowers are easy to grow. They are self-reproducing, resilient, hardy, beautiful, and well-adapted to our climate and soil. Once they have established themselves, that is true, but they are not all self-perpetuating. I had tried to grow wildflowers in rich soil which was a fundamental mistake. Wildflowers thrive in poor soil. The initial effort required in setting up a wildflower garden is considerably more than setting up a perennial border or equivalent task. This is the apparent paradox: truly wild plants need lots of care and attention. Good soil will need to be degraded so that it will appeal to wildflowers.

Wild Flowers- Dominant 'Campanula'

Areas of your garden that are neglected and difficult to maintain should be ideal. It helps if the plot only receives partial sun and, to start with, all existing vegetation is removed.

Controlling weeds is crucial, and you get to decide which to keep or remove. Initially, the removal of unwanted vegetation and clumps is best done manually. The next step is to kill weeds and vegetation by solarisation which involves lots of watering. Then cover the area with securely pegged transparent plastic sheeting for up to two months. Periodically remove the dead material.

Now the soil needs to be made ready through shallow tilling of the top three or four inches rather than mechanically rotavating, which may well disturb the ground too much. Level the soil and then rake. Seeds will need to be placed in grooves in the raked soil, and the preparation of your wildflower garden is then nearing completion. A combination of seeds and plants is probably desirable. The following plants will attract butterflies and other insects: dandelions, dill, Black-eyed Susan, lemon balm, yarrow, zinnia, cornflower, amaranths, clover, and nasturtium. If you prefer, plants that attract beneficial insects or beneficial bugs include bishop's weed, fennel, crocus, honeysuckle, foxgloves, viper's bugloss, sedums, and hellebore. Some of the above examples will be mainstream plants as well as wildflowers.

Your entire garden ecosystem will need the three main categories of beneficial insects: pollinators, parasites, and predators. Organic pest control is greatly assisted by ladybirds beetles which prey on aphids, whitefly, and mites; ground beetles prey on slugs and caterpillars; green lacewings eat aphids, whiteflies, and mealybugs; damsel bugs prey on caterpillars, mites, and aphids. Other beneficial bugs are parasitic wasps, moths, solitary bees, spiders, the common wasp, bumblebees, and centipedes.

Be in no doubt we are talking bug wars here. Both wildflower gardens and cultivated sections of gardens need as much help as they can get in defending themselves against bugs intent on consuming your garden's contents. We are back here to some fundamental aspects of gardening aesthetics and rewards. You are, in effect, the manager, and where invasive insects and diseases are concerned, you are the general in charge of defence. Your physical efforts reward you, helping to keep you fit and limbered up and enjoying the literal fruits of your labour in vegetables and fruit.

It is aesthetically pleasing to plan and maintain a diverse garden in which plants and flowers provide beauty and solace. It is rewarding to make decisions that promote organic solutions to pests and a holistic sense of the balance of nature. You gain from the satisfaction obtained from maximising the benefits to yourself, your family, and your friends. Planning, watering, digging, weeding, and planting can be enjoyed as part of this venture. Failure can be learned from, and mistakes can be rectified. In a very real way, gardens are heuristic. They, like any hobby or interest, help us discover and learn about ourselves. Problem-solving and self-discovery are all part and parcel of the adventure called gardening.

All parts of our gardens provide spiritual meaning. The symbolism recurs with the seasons. Spring and summer see the springing back to life, the sprouting of growth, in the growing seasons. Plant life is resurrected. The waning that comes with winter, the death of garden life, and the lack of light in the northern hemisphere are replaced by increasing amounts of light, new growth, life, and optimism. Research has shown that even a twenty-minute exposure to nature's greenery is restorative: mood levels improve; sunlight provides a feel-good boost and vitamins D and C. The absorption of gardening that comes from physical activity displaces some of the anxieties and stresses we suffer from modern life. Working outdoors allows us to shelve our problems for a while and regain some helpful perspective on our lives. The disconnect from nature that city life creates can be bridged.

Your garden can provide two models of design: disorder or chance order in the wildflower garden and order in the cultivated garden with its more regimented lines. Your senses will be engaged in different ways. Both can create sensory stimuli. Your connection to life will be different. The basic sense of sight will be rewarded by the harmony of your planned garden and the more individual expression of wildness finding its own order in the wildflower patch. Smell, sound, touch, and taste will also differ, but both areas of your garden will give you mindfulness. The beauty of your creation will be tailored to your needs. It can always be enhanced, enlarged, or reduced as you wish.

As mentioned above, the country garden look is halfway in appearance between a formal garden with its regular lines of carefully pruned bushes, neat hedging, uniform borders, water features, and seating under archways. The country garden has flowing, undulating lines of massed flowers swaying in the gentlest breeze. It has a more natural appearance though it is artfully created, and, of course, we associate it with the sounds of industrious insects, especially the buzzing of bees as they collect nectar from the flowers. Such a garden is a visual feast, and if you can, use plants that are native to your area, which will minimise the need for chemicals.

Chapter Eight: Wildlife in the Garden

Wildlife in the garden and wildflower gardens touch on so many similar themes and issues. We, in our gardens, replicate how we feel about life in general: a manicured hedge, immaculate flower borders, pristine summerhouse and shed, well-maintained paths, and geometric designs everywhere will not offer much to a wide range of wildlife or host wildflower areas. If we want wildlife in our gardens, it needs to be encouraged and planned for just like wildflowers. Your personality is at the heart of your garden. Up to a quarter of a city's area can be made up of a patchwork of gardens in the context of nearby nature reserves, green spaces, and countryside.

Of course, how much wildlife you can attract depends on where you live, how much you want to accommodate, and what you would prefer to keep out. Early this morning, I saw four pigeons chasing each other on the grass; a squirrel was hanging upside down, taking seed from the bird feeder while a neighbour's rat scurried back and forth close to the low wall. To some, this would be nirvana; to others a cause for concern. Rats are feared for historical reasons because of their reputation as disease carriers, but if they are not intrusive, it is possible to live with them. Brown rats are omnivorous, eating pretty much anything, from fruit and seeds to human food waste, insects, birds' eggs, or even small mammals. My philosophy is simple: I do not have the right to kill what I cannot create. The exceptions would be the need for self-defence against any insect or animal that attacked me or my family and visitors. Where possible, however, I believe we should co-exist with nature. If any wild animal threatens your health or well-being, there are experts in 'pest' control who can be called upon.

The benefits of a garden that hosts wildlife can be seen and heard all year round, but how do we achieve this natural outdoor space? It helps if we can provide homes and habitats for our garden residents. Firstly, stop tidying up everywhere in the autumn. Leave the untidy-looking stems of perennials for ladybird beetles [a Coccinellidae beetle] to help them over the winter. Uncut seed heads will supply food to birds. Insects of all sorts will live in piles of garden refuse, such as plant stems, leaves, and grass which can gather in less-used areas.

Hibernating, endangered hedgehogs overwinter in such natural refuges, and it is good practice to check garden waste before lighting bonfires in case there are dormant hedgehogs. Importantly, we need to reconsider the function of creatures like slugs. Rather than reach for a container of 'Slug Death', view slugs and snails as an intrinsic part of the garden's cycle of food provision for frogs, toads, and hedgehogs. If you must limit the slug and snail population, avoid pellets containing methiocarb or metaldehyde. These ingredients will enter the food chain; pellets containing ferrous sulphate will not. Gritty sand or crushed eggshells will deter without killing. Of course, the worlds of birds, plants, and animals are interlinked, so by attracting or keeping one species; others are also attracted. Declining species such as hedgehogs, song thrushes, sparrows, and stag beetles will all benefit from managed wildlife gardens, bringing movement, colour, and variety. Greenflies and blackflies can be tackled with diluted household detergent without harming other insects.

It is very helpful for wildlife if the soil is well mulched in the spring and autumn, as this helps the garden absorb heavy downpours in winter and minimise flooding. One very important soil issue is the use of peat-free composts and mulches. Try to use alternatives to peat, such as chipped bark, coir, or leaf mould. We need to preserve UK peat bogs which are important habitats for wildlife. There may be similar concerns about which type of soil to use where you live. There is excellent guidance online about composting, and it is an excellent way of recycling food waste, garden waste, the contents of the vacuum cleaner, and even card and shredded paper.

Water features, such as wildlife ponds, are very important and have been given a separate chapter.

The creation and maintenance of your own wildlife space depend on four fundamental elements: a variety of planting, water, deadwood, and trees. Wildlife will thrive in your garden if these features are introduced. You will be creating a haven for yourself and wildlife.

The use of space everywhere can be utilised. The only limit is your imagination in enrolling roofs, walls, gaps, and small spaces. Makeshift ponds in old sinks cut down containers, and old buckets can become home to teeming wildlife. Small gravel gardens or paved areas can become home to scabious, a nectar-providing perennial. Butterflies cannot resist nectar plants like marjoram and lavender planted in all sorts and shapes of a container, including window boxes. Night-scented stocks and tobacco plants will lure moths. You only need to provide the basics for your wildlife: a breeding place, shelter, water, and food. Let us pursue this in more detail.

Compost heaps and bins turn garden waste into natural fertiliser while providing overwintering habitats for hedgehogs and small mammals. The shelter is also provided by crevices and cracks in walls and rockeries, the sort of nooks and crannies beloved of solitary bees and spiders.

Wall-growing plants that provide cover and shelter include wallflowers, various ferns, ivy-leaved toadflax, and red valerian. Another ad hoc shelter can be provided by a pile of logs situated in a shady corner.

It will be another good site for hibernating hedgehogs. Beetle larvae will feed there, and animals such as slow worms, frogs, and toads will shelter.

The feeder that attracted the squirrel in the introduction to this chapter provides seed, but nuts and fat balls are also dispensed by feeders or can be left on trays or the ground. Mealworms are eaten by insect predators. The feeding area should be moved periodically and cleansed to guard against disease, predators, and rodents. Bird boxes with varied size openings for different birds are a good solution to targeting the birds you want to feed: nuthatches and sparrows need 32 cm. while tits will require a 28 mm. entrance hole. Some species, like robins, prefer an open-fronted design. The boxes need to be sited out of the full sun and out of reach of predators using nearby branches.

Zones of interest might include the creation of a butterfly garden. We have already seen the role containers can play in providing nectar-rich flowers. Plant verbena and ice plant as well. Cottage garden flowers in a sheltered sunny spot will be attractive and nectar-giving. You could be very discriminating and plan different areas to attract different butterfly species: the painted lady likes thistles; brimstone eats alder buckthorn and purging buckthorn; large and small whites like wild and cultivated cabbages; green-veined white and orange tips eat lady's smock, hedge garlic, and hedge mustard; the common blue likes bird's foot trefoil. Large skipper, marbled white, gatekeeper, and meadow brown feast on Yorkshire fog, meadow grass, false brome, and cocksfoot. Evergreens such as ivy, buddleia (known as the butterfly bush), and fruit trees will all add diversity to your garden and provide plentiful sources of nectar and shelter. Hedges, such as hawthorn, privet, wild rose, holly, hazel, and elder, create food and living spaces, while pyracantha and berberis produce berries for birds. The caterpillars of butterflies such as red admiral, tortoiseshell, and peacock feed on nettles. Plant the nettles in a sunny place, as butterflies are not keen on laying their eggs in shady places.

The seasonal food cycle for butterflies for nectar-giving plants is that in spring, they feed on primrose, aubretia, and sweet rocket; in summer, it is lavender, buddleia, knapweed, red valerian, heliotrope, cat mint, and thyme; in autumn it is ice-plant, hyssop, Michaelmas daisy, and sweet scabious.

Native trees that attract wildlife include dogwood, bird cherry, crab apple, juniper, rowan, willow, and ash. Bushes such as broom, dog rose, alder buckthorn, and guelder rose to do the same. Where you live will determine the size and complexion of your garden. You want as many frogs, toads, birds, and small mammals like hedgehogs and bats as you can attract. They all eat slugs and insects. Hoverflies, ladybirds, and lacewings eat aphids. Nesting and roosting sites for birds can also be provided by climbing plants like quince and honeysuckle, which are also a haven for small animals and insects.

Many online sites provide excellent advice on how to attract wildlife that a swift internet search will produce. Try: How to make a bee hotel; How to make a log shelter; How to build a hedgehog home; How to build a bat box; How to attract bumblebees to your garden; How to attract pollinators; How to build a bug mansion.

If an attractive animal decides to visit you, it can be great fun to study it, especially if it stays for some months. Here is the true tale of a lone rabbit for you to enjoy. We took advantage of its presence to have a 'Name the rabbit competition'.

He, probably a young buck forced to leave the colony, took up residence under the shed at the end of the garden. The Annual Summer Party seemed the ideal occasion to decide on a name for him. Entries from far and wide were submitted, and party-goers voted for the winning name. Male and female names were allowed by the ever-tolerant judge. The entries for the resident rabbit were Sheddie; Sir

Freddie of Fifty-One; Thumper; Gandalf; Matilda; Lapinlou [this from France]; Killer; Captain Carrot; Rebus; Barry; Beryl; Sir Fluffikins; Countess; Mr Waabit; Bigfoot; Artemis; Hop Cross Bunny; Aphrodite; Kev; Hermes and Snoopy. The winner of a fiercely fought competition was Captain Carrot.

Captain Carrot deepened his burrow under the shed as autumn approached. He did several keep-fit sessions starting as early as 7:00 am and intermittently throughout the day. His routine included chasing the birds, including magpies, with whom he performed a kind of dance, shadow boxing, and a type of Zen routine whereby he faced my neighbour's fence for many reflective minutes, sometimes raising his front legs in supplication. He also practised fox evasion by doing sprints.

Captain Carrot

The Captain ignored two carrots which I bought at great expense, as well as food pellets and fresh straw for his burrow. Sadly, Captain Carrot left his home under the shed and never returned. We assume he went off to find a mate. We still miss him. He was not a pet but a fun part of the extended family.

Less dramatic examples of local wildlife visitors to our garden include frogs, toads, house mice, wood mice, the brown rat mentioned earlier, and huge numbers of different types of birds. The insect population in our garden is highly divergent and populous. By the nearby river and in the adjacent wetlands, you will see voles, currently herons nesting in a local tree, the common shrew, and grass and water snakes. Now, despite seeing many red foxes at night on the local roads, and as far as we know, they have ignored us. We do not have chickens or other such temptations, and our food waste bins are secure, so this highly successful scavenger goes elsewhere. Some people find them very unwelcome visitors; some consider them beautiful. They sensibly rarely go near humans. You are only likely to see rarer wildlife, such as badgers, polecats, stoats, weasels, brown hares, harvest mice, moles, roe, and muntjac deer if your garden opens onto fields or woodlands.

If you have children, your garden can be a major educational resource. Your children could keep a seasonal video diary of the life cycle, be responsible for a part of the garden, manage the bird feeding and monitor what is happening with you as a team. Their outdoor time will be invaluable and enjoyable. If they start young, their interest may survive adolescence. There are some 22,400 species of insects in Britain and some 91,000 in the USA, with some estimated 73,000 undescribed. Worldwide the figure is about 900,000 known species! Terry Irwin of the Smithsonian Institute estimates between 2 and 30 million. Only about 1% are pests.

Carpet of pale-yellow roses

Chapter Nine: The Water Garden

Environmentalists all recommend the use of water in the garden, and there is no doubt that water adds an extra dimension to any space. This may be as little as a bird bath, a saucer of water on a balcony for birds and creatures to drink, or a full-blown wildlife pond. Making a pond in the garden is an easy way of helping us to connect with nature while providing a haven for water life and is part of the food chain for wildlife in general. This is increasingly important as we deal with the rapid loss of natural habitats, and careful thought in construction and design will all contribute to creating both the perfect environment and another restorative and fascinating aspect of gardening.

At this point, it is vital to think about safety. Children are at risk from both deep and shallow water, and if you have a young family or young visitors, then it is worth investing in a rigid safety grille that can be removed when danger is over.

Water features can play an important role in any garden, both as a focal point and in providing a home and sustenance for wildlife. They provide ornamental interest, soothing sound, and natural habitat. Fountains, always spectacular and delightful, need a water supply and power, but this requirement does not apply to all water features. Solar power is a solution. Whatever you choose, the sound is one of the sought-after features: babbling, trickling, tinkling, lapping, rippling, and splashing, and animate your surroundings. Add the attraction to wildlife, and its relevance becomes complete. Moving water has to be pumped, and many people opt for that facility. Alternatively, ponds can be topped up from a hosepipe or rainfall from a water butt.

Many off-the-shelf devices have self-contained water supplies, needing only occasional topping up. Or you can make your very own water feature with whatever water supply it needs. Whichever you choose, the siting is important: cleaning out ponds and water items is sometimes essential, so avoid placing them under trees. Many people like to site their features in a natural context surrounded by plants, bushes, and flowers. Taste in materials will determine whether you create a modern or traditional look. Mesmerising water sounds can be created in designs in metal, stainless steel, and glass which will complement a modern design, while terracotta and stone are ideal for traditional styles. Old artefacts like millstones and troughs can be acquired as decorative features. Pouring jug water features such as terracotta olive jars have a traditional ambience. Craft-made jugs with a hole for the pump to easily slot into are easy to source, and they can be either individual features that empty into a bowl or used to create rills to pour into a pond. Such features can be centred in different plantings. Lighting will affect mood in the evening and is well worth investing in as an additional enhancing feature.

Making a wildlife pond is not that difficult. It could be as simple as buying a pre-formed pond or a half barrel or tub sunk into the ground. If you are digging a pond, first decide on the shape, depth, design, and size you prefer, but the deeper, the better. Careful thought about design and construction is well worth the extra effort. Remember to make a deep zone, a shallow area, and a ledge for marginal plants. A good idea is to have a slope at one side, with pebbles, so that birds can drink and bathe safely and small animals, like hedgehogs, can escape should they accidentally fall in or baby frogs can leave the pond to begin their independent life. Once dug, any sharp roots or stones need to be removed before spreading a thick layer of sand at the bottom, or maybe recycle an old piece of carpet, to protect the butyl liner. Drape your liner over the hole, weigh the edges, and trim to the right size. Decide whether you want hard landscaping at the edge or maybe some turf, and you are ready to fill the liner. It is possible to buy turfs with meadow plants already planted, which can look very natural, but arrangements of rocks or patio stones can look equally attractive.

It is sensible to use the advice of aquatic retailers. They are always knowledgeable and eager to help and will advise about fountains should you want to install one. The sound of trickling water, as mentioned before, is calming and therapeutic and is another part of the sensory aspect of gardening. Fountains can be simple or elaborate, depending on your budget and the size of the pond. If you don't want the expense of installing an electric pump, there are, as referred to above, solar alternatives. Fountains help to increase the oxygen in ponds, so they are not only decorative but functional too. The pond can look aesthetically pleasing by using decorative solar lighting around its edges and is another encouragement to take in the summer air as the evenings lengthen with its increasing opportunities to use the garden as an extra room for food, drinks, and socialising. Health-giving summer scents and natural warmth are precious resources before the cooler and darker evenings draw in.

The best time to plant a pond is in the spring or early summer. The water is warming up, the spring rain can help to fill the area and encourage aquatic creatures, and it is a good time to plant. Informal ponds are fairly low maintenance once the balance between plant and insect life has had time to establish. You will need to watch for algae, particularly until the recommended 50 to 70% of the surface area is covered by plants. The smaller the pond, the more the problem. Sunlight encourages algae, but there are successful and safe products that deal with this problem quickly and will not harm wildlife. In a more formal pool where the focus is purely decorative, with no plants or wildlife features, algae will be much more of a problem.

Blanket weed which grows in strands under the surface of the water often appears in periods of high sunshine and is easily removed by hand. A good tip is to curl it around a small cane, a bit like making candyfloss. The blanket weed will compost down if you have a compost heap but always leave the plant debris at the side of the pond until any creatures can make their way back into the water. Duckweed is another annoyance and can quickly take over the surface of a small pond. It is well worth buying a small net to 'fish' and remove the offending weed regularly. Water snails can be a problem, too, as they tend to eat the plants, but they can also feast on decaying matter, so just keep an eye on their numbers. They can often be found underwater lily leaves and easily removed if they become a pest.

Autumn is a good time to tidy up, and plants do need thinning from time to time as their growth through the summer can be rapid. It is satisfying to see a neat pond and decide whether to change plants or restock. Once the plants have been thinned, they can be replanted in pond pots and covered with gravel to keep the soil in place. It is sensible to remove fallen leaves and flowers as they can sour the water, and netting can be bought cheaply from garden centres to keep the pond surface clear in the autumn. It is easy to weigh down the netting with large stones or bricks.

As the winter approaches, it is a good opportunity to clean the filters and remove pumps – they can be damaged if the water freezes – and to pack them away until the spring. An easy way of keeping the pond from freezing and possibly putting the wildlife at risk is to pop a small rubber ball in the water, which can be removed, leaving an ice-free spot.

Often, in February, my less-than-intelligent frogs can spawn before the autumn netting has been removed, and in frosty weather, the spawn doesn't develop as it should. When spawn does develop, it is fascinating to watch the embryos enclosed in jelly begin to change shape and then to see the metamorphosis from tadpole to frog. The rear and then the front legs grow, the tail shortens, and hopefully, the baby frog will become an adult, ready for the cycle to begin again. On summer evenings, when the garden doors are still open to catch the last sunshine and warmth, frogs have been known to come into the house. Returning them to their natural home is easier said than done! Toads, frogs, and newts feed on the land but need water to survive, mate, and lay their eggs. The pond will have natural predators. Birds, dragonfly larvae, water boatmen, and snakes all feed on spawn, but plants on the surface can provide protection. Try not to disturb the spawn and never share it as it can spread the disease called Chytrids which is a skin fungus and fatal to frogs.

Ponds teem with life as a quick supervised dip with the children, and a jam jar will testify. Within a very short time of making a wildlife pond, dragonflies appear, water boatmen skate across the surface, and bees and wasps come down to drink. Birds love to bathe and satisfy their thirst. Frogs, toads, and newts seem to have a sixth sense and are quick to take up residence. On one memorable occasion, there was great excitement in my garden when we discovered a shed skin from a grass snake, presumably visiting in search of food and hungry for a frog. Dragonflies, mayflies or damselflies, caddis flies, pond skaters, and water beetles all breed in water, and the birds can pick off the insects.

As elsewhere in the garden, personal taste dictates the type of plants you choose. Choose carefully for the size of your pond, as some plants can be invasive. Submerged oxygenating plants are vitally important to keep the pond healthy, to keep the water clarified, and to suppress algae. One of my favourite pond plants is the golden yellow marsh marigold which sits on the margins and, in the spring, heralds the promise of summer sunshine. Other lovely plants for the margins are the purple, yellow, or white irises and the bright red stemmed lobelia with its colourful red flowers. Pale blue water forget-me-nots float on the surface, and the sedges create upright interest in the margins.

Water mint provides scent, and the stunning white flowers of the arum lily are an exotic addition to the shallows. In larger ponds, bullrushes are another interesting plant, and the beautiful water lilies, the nymphaea, reminiscent of a Monet[1] painting with their multi colours, are a beautiful addition. Water lilies can grow very large, and for small ponds, there are miniature varieties, so research is an important part of your planting. Some companies provide plant kits, but these can be expensive to buy. It is always wise to visit gardens with established ponds and aquatic garden centres and make a note of what appeals to you and what will fit into your wildlife pond. Ask friends who are thinning plants for pieces which will be reminders of times shared and save money too.

Above all, enjoy your pond: the wildlife haven you have made. Watch the environment develop and benefit from the calming sensory effects of water and nature, whatever the season.

---

[1] Claude Monet- 1840-1926- French impressionist painter

Rose New Dawn

Chapter Ten: Floriography – The Language of Flower

Flowers have been used for centuries in art, myths, and literature and in biblical references to symbolise emotion and add layers of meaning. In *Hamlet,* Ophelia used flowers to emphasise her distress, and Millais' painting of her watery grave has evoked soulful reflection. Eve, the stereotypical symbol of original sin, will always be associated with the apple and temptation.

In sentimental Victorian times, when expressing one's feelings publicly was not encouraged or considered poor etiquette, the term **Floriography** was invented as a means for using flowers as a form of communicating emotions instead of words. The need for secret communication is perhaps less important nowadays, but red roses on Valentine's Day are a notable exception.

Recently I found a worn and tiny volume called *The Language of Flowers*[2]. The previous owner has written the date 1904 on the front, so it has its roots in the Victorian era. The introduction suggests that 'the flower world is linked with all the finer sympathies of our nature' and that flowers are relevant from young love to old age and the sorrows of death. The language is certainly very flowery and is interspersed with poetry and hundreds of plants, many of which seem obscure in today's gardens. Some of the meanings given are contradictory, even in the same plant, which could have created mixed messages and misunderstandings, while some of the meanings are not flattering: the basil for hatred and the buttercup for ingratitude.

In keeping with the therapeutic focus of this book, I have included some of the plants mentioned in previous chapters, with meanings referring to the body, mind, and spirit. The suggestions might provide ideas for planting schemes or

---

[2] *The Language of Flowers*, adapted from *The Language and Sentiment of Flowers*, London: Frederick Warne and Co.

gifts of flowers, but a withered bouquet is not recommended for obvious reasons, and some cultures view colours differently, so a little bit of research is a good idea.

When choosing flower colours, generally, red is for love and passion, pink for innocence and grace, yellow is for happiness and friendship, and white is for purity. There seems to be a coloured rose for just about any occasion, a special wedding anniversary, a birthday, or to offer consolation, which makes a bunch of roses, or maybe the gift of a bush to grow in the garden, an enduring message of love, congratulation or sympathy. Somewhat confusingly, the book also lists rose meanings ranging from pleasure to shame, danger to charm, and virtue to beauty, but a bouquet of roses in today's more realistic world is simply a special present. Meanings can depend on the number of blooms or even the method of giving. One rose suggests love at first sight, while fifty suggests the donor needs to look impressive! A bouquet offered upside down is a sign of rejection, and one in the right hand is a 'yes'.

The scented sweet pea is suggested as a symbol of gratitude, while white lilies offer sympathy and the regeneration of the soul. Lavender symbolises devotion and sincerity, and the bright, emotive red poppy will always be known as the flower of remembrance and consolation. Jasmine, another highly scented plant, suggests joy, beauty, and sensuality, and the sunflower adoration. Ivy is for fidelity and marriage, and the snowdrop offers hopes that marital union will be the outcome. Almond flowers also offer hope, bluebell constancy, and broom humility. The crocus, one of the first flowers of the spring, suggests youthful gladness.

Ironically, the prickly cactus was considered a symbol of warmth, while the beautiful camellia symbolised loveliness and perfection. Forget-me-nots are self-explanatory and, as an early spring flower, can be a pleasurable reminder of friendships past and present. Geraniums can signify true friendship, comfort, and steadfastness; the highly scented honeysuckle devoted affection. The Narcissus is a lovely, delicately scented plant and one to cheer after the dark days of winter. I am happy to enjoy it for that, but the myth of Narcissus suggests egotism. Most of the flowers have alternative meanings, but the Narcissus will always be associated with an arrogant youth!

The olive brings peace and the daisy patience and/or innocence, and the colourful petunias suggest that 'your patience soothes me'. Rosemary is for remembrance, rudbeckia justice, and the shamrock or clover, light-heartedness: the elusive four-leaf clover is asking 'be mine'. Basil, a lovely summer herb, sends good wishes and sage domestic virtue. The red tulip offers declarations of love, a variegated tulip with beautiful eyes but the yellow? – hopeless love. The apple is, of course, seen as an object of temptation, and for the Victorians, orange blossom, still popular for brides, announced that one's purity equals one's loveliness. Who knew that rhubarb offered them advice and gooseberry anticipation?

The book gives examples of suggested bouquets. In the spring, primroses and daisies are for the protection of youth and maternal love. The summer gives declarations of love with ivy, jasmine, and myrtle. The autumn bouquet contains poppies and thrift and offers sympathy and consolation. Wintery holly and mistletoe give hope that difficulties will be surmounted.

There are plants asking questions and plants providing answers, but if in doubt, the snapdragon is offering a simple 'no' and the striped carnation, a refusal. Who could resist a peach tree stating that 'your charms are unequalled', but this could be negated by the foxglove, which suggests insincerity.

Floriography, it appears, can be a romantic minefield perhaps, while regretting the loss of the quirkiness of flowers as a means of communication, growing and giving flowers and plants simply to express love, thanks, sympathy, and friendship in the colours you love, and the scents they provide is our best caring modern-day practice and one promoted by the essence of this book.

Olive Tree in a Large Terracotta Pot

Chapter Eleven: Types of Soil

Why is soil so important in gardening? Until we get serious about gardening, the answer will be vague: obviously, it is a medium for growing things. However, the soil is a complex mixture of organisms, minerals, liquids, and gases, and you need to know how to create the optimum soil for your growing needs.

There are six main soil groups: clay, sandy, silty, peaty, chalky, and loamy, but the three main soil types are **loam, clay,** and **sandy**. What type of soil are you working with? To find out, buy a pH testing kit from your local garden centre. The pH level is defined as the acidity level of your soil. The more neutral the soil is, the better will be the growth of your plants. Some varieties of plants require a more acidic medium, but most plants need neutral pH to grow.

Loam is ideal for growing plants as it has a balanced portion of pH, organic matter, and a crumbly texture. It drains the water from the soil as well as retaining moisture. Flower bulbs that grow well in sandy soils include snowdrops, anemones, grape hyacinths, lilies, and daffodils. Annual and perennial flowers recommended for sandy loam soils include lemon balm, sage, sunflowers, and poppies. All fruit and vegetable crops benefit from loam soil.

Clay soil is heavy, sticky, and difficult to work with but can be improved by adding organic matter. It does have advantages as it maintains moisture. However, it can bake hard in the summer and become 'claggy' in the winter. Plants that thrive in clay soil include rambling roses, climbing roses, shrubs, species roses, foxgloves, lilies, sambuca, hydrangeas, euphorbia, and persicaria.

Sandy soil is easier to handle than clay soil, but it comes with other problems. For example, it drains fast and retains fewer nutrients. Plants that thrive in sandy soils include salvia, lavender, sedum, buddleia, the rose of Sharon, and Mediterranean herbs.

Weeding is a task that is not everyone's favourite, but it is important as weeds will take nutrients from the soil and, therefore, your plants. Whether your soil is low in nutrients, has poor drainage, or is sandy, it deteriorates over time and needs to be refreshed and made healthier by adding organic matter. Well-rotted compost, leaf mould from the autumn tidying, shop-bought or home created, is the best solution, and mulch is an excellent way of keeping the weeds down. Remember, as mentioned in the wildlife chapter, if buying your compost, it is really important to choose peat-free bags to protect the environment. Look at the labels.

Adding compost will introduce microorganisms that will improve your soil by breaking down the organic matter. You can add as much and as often as you like. You can add it before and during the planting season, and you will quickly notice the benefits in the development of your plants. If you have space for a compost heap, grass clippings, shredded autumn leaves, straw, woodchips, vegetable peelings, and garden waste will rot down to give you free fertiliser, which will help increase fertility, water retention and improve the texture of your soil. Don't add animal products that can encourage vermin. If you are buying compost, there are special types for every need. Ask the experts at the garden centres and check the packaging. Remember, compost and mulches are important, but plants also need light, air, and water to thrive.

Purple Azalea

Chapter Twelve: In Conclusion

"Nature is a teacher whose wisdom we can learn, and without which any human life is vain and incomplete." William Wordsworth

I have heard it said that treating plants like one's offspring is a good gardening habit. Plants don't have temper tantrums or teenage angst, but they do respond to nurture as they develop, and they do respond to love and care. Some advocate talking to plants which they swear makes a difference. Everything is debatable, and anything is worth a try. Good husbandry, like weeding, watering, staking, feeding, and the all-important advice that the right plants are in the right space will all add to your success. Prevention is better than cure.

Be warned, gardening is an ever-learning journey that can become more than a hobby and become an obsession. It knows no boundaries, and regardless of culture, age or ethnicity, it promotes vitality, creative artistry, and makes memories. It promotes intergenerational bonding and the passing on of traditions and is a great pastime, whatever your space. From toddlers to teens and into retirement, there are opportunities for family gardening.

Young children love the different textures, watching things grow, watching the insects, and playing in mud: mud kitchens are a popular addition to early years education, and caring for plants and wildlife teaches responsibility, self-confidence, and the issues of cause and effect.

Given the right incentives, teenagers can be encouraged to leave their technical devices and engage in gardening activities – even if it is only to help make space to kick a ball, dig a plot or a pond, harvest the produce, or spend time with friends. They are excellent at the minefield of internet plant searches.

The middle years are enhanced by growing food, learning new skills, relaxing under a shady tree after a hard day's work, and socialising with friends in the fresh air in the space you have created. It is great exercise and cheaper than a gym membership! Sunlight increases Vitamin D, creating healthy bones that are important in later life.

Gardening is a goal for retirement, maintaining mental and physical activity for health, although it is important to recognise physical limitations. It can be done from a wheelchair with adapted tools and is a stimulus for those with sensory impairment. It provides texture, taste, the sounds of water, rustling leaves and birdsong, colour, and beauty.

It is a therapy for dementia sufferers, boosting mood and well-being. For those with mental health difficulties, exercise and fresh air increase serotonin so important for elevating mood. Therapeutic gardening can be prescribed by general practitioners and is a great stress reliever, lowering anxiety and panic attacks. There is something unique about the natural world and its ability to heal: its ability to offer peace, calmness, and balance.

Community gardening is on the increase, creating opportunities for the lonely to mix, meet, and share experiences, memories, and homegrown produce. It gives a reason to leave the house and is an opportunity to make new friends.

Above all, experience and sharing teach gardeners the tricks for success. Keep updated by reading articles, newsletters, internet searches, and books. The more you learn and garden, the greater the benefits.

Art, poetry, and music have all been inspired by the beauty of the natural world. Frank Lloyd Wright (1867 – 1959), the American architect, designer, and educator, wrote: 'Nature is the inspiration for all ornamentation' and 'Study nature, love nature, and stay close to nature'. They are both mantras to aid our mindfulness and well-being. Enjoy your gardening journey, however big or small, and stay close to the healing spirit of nature.

Norbury Park in Surrey in the Afternoon Sun

Appendix

Fruit In The Garden

Where To Grow

traditional bed

raised bed

undercover

containers

hanging baskets

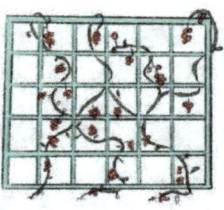
walls & fences

How To Prune A Tree

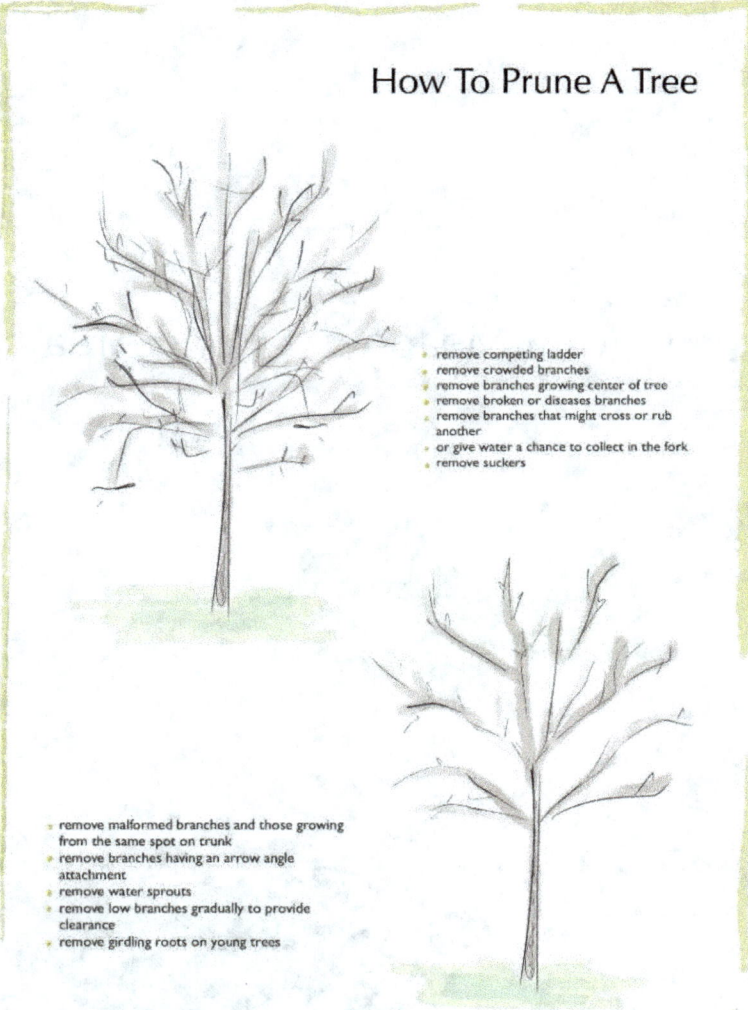

- remove competing ladder
- remove crowded branches
- remove branches growing center of tree
- remove broken or diseases branches
- remove branches that might cross or rub another
- or give water a chance to collect in the fork
- remove suckers

- remove malformed branches and those growing from the same spot on trunk
- remove branches having an arrow angle attachment
- remove water sprouts
- remove low branches gradually to provide clearance
- remove girdling roots on young trees

Mini Meadow & Pond Area

Bibliography

Bird, Richard, *200 Great Perennials*, London: Hamlyn, (2009)

Bolton, Polly, *The Cottage Garden*, Bristol: Parragon Books, (1996)

Don, Monty, *My Garden World,* London: Two Roads, (2020)

Gault, S. Millar, *The Dictionary of Shrubs in Colour*, London: Rainbird Publishing Group Ltd., (1984)

Hay, Roy, and Synge, Patrick M., *The Color Dictionary of Flowers and Plants for Home and Garden,* New York: Crown Publishers Inc., (1972)

McHoy, Peter, *The Practical Book of Small Gardens,* London: Anness Publishing Limited, (2001)

McVicar, J., *A Pocketful of Herbs,* London: Bloomsbury Absolute, (2019)

Spence, Ian, *Gardening Through the Year,* London: Dorling Kindersley (2001)

The Language of Flowers, Warnes Bijou Books, London: Frederick Warne & Co., (c.1904)

The RHS Gardeners' Encyclopedia of Plants and Flowers, London: Dorling Kindersley, (1990)

Webb, A, and Craze, R, *The Herb and Spice Companion*, London: Quantum Publishing Ltd. (2003)

Index

1
1837 coronation, 44

2
22,400 species of insects in Britain, 78

A
a new gardening year, 38

adiponectin, 44

algae, 82, 85

allium, 27

allotment, 48

Almond flowers, 90

amaranths, 65

America, 44

ancient Egypt, 44

angelica, 60

antioxidants, 40, 42, 43, 44, 51, 52

aphids, 33, 48, 66, 75

apples, 35, 43

Apples, pears, cherries and plums, 42

Aristotle (c.272-287 B.C.), 55

Arrangements of pots, 48

artificial grass, 13

arum lily, 86

as nature's anti-biotic, 51

aubergines, 47

autumn crocus, 35

azalea, 18

B
badgers, 77

bargains, 28

basil, 18, 60, 88

Basil, 57, 60, 90

bay laurel, 60

bay leaves, 58

beetroot, 48

Berberis Darwinii, 27

bird feeder, 69

birds, 16, 20, 27, 33, 34, 36, 40, 64, 70, 71, 73, 74, 75, 76, 77, 79, 81, 85

Birds, 36, 48, 84, 85

bishop's weed, 65

blackberries, 39, 41

Blackberries, 41

blackcurrants, 42

Black-eyed Susan, 65

blackfly, 71

blackthorn trees [Prunus spinosa], 41

blanket weed, 83
Blanket weed, 83
blood pressure, 39
blood sugar levels, 44
bluebell, 90
bluebells, 27
blueberries, 39
Blueberries, 40
Broccoli, 51
brown hares, 77
Buddleia, 34
buddleia [the butterfly bush], 17
bumblebees, 66, 75
butterflies, 16, 17, 34, 64, 65, 74

C

cactus, 90
caddis flies, 85
callistemon [bottle brush], 18
camellia, 90
camellias, 19, 25
carbohydrates, 50
Carrots, 51
caterpillars, 66, 74
celeriac, 48
centipedes, 66
chamomile lawn, 61
cherry, apple and almond trees, 26
chillies, 47, 48
China, 44

chipped bark, 71
chives, 18, 60
cholesterol, 39, 40, 43
chrysanthemums, 36
Chytrids, 85
cider or apple juice, 43
Clay, 94
clematis, 27, 29, 34
clover, 65, 90
comfrey, 60
Commercial herbs and supplements, 54
common wasp, 66
Community gardening, 98
compost, 42, 49, 51, 83, 94, 95
composting, 71
concept areas, 13
container, 34, 45, 48, 50, 60, 70, 72
cordials, 42
cordon and espalier fruit trees, 14
cornflower, 65
cosmos, 29
cottage garden, 14, 15, 47
cowslips, 57
cress, 52
crocus, 65, 90
Crocus bulbs, 25
cucumbers, 48
Culpeper, 55

Cyclamen, 24

D

daffodils, 25, 26, 93
dahlias, 35
damsel bugs, 66
damselflies, 85
dandelions, 65
Deadheading, 34
deadwood, 72
deciduous trees, 27
dill, 65
dividing walls, 20
Dragonflies, 85
drought, 15, 48, 49

E

eating less meat, 46
echinacea, 34
Euonymous Silver Queen, 25
euonymus, 20
Europe, 44, 55
excessive heat, 48

F

feeding in spring to boost harvests, 41
fennel, 60, 65
fibre, 40, 41, 43, 44, 52
fight infection and viruses, 42
Floriography, 87, 91
folk-legend the Devil stamps, 41

forget-me-nots, 86
Forsythia, 25
fountain, 17
Fountains, 79, 82
foxgloves, 57, 65, 94
fragrance, aroma and flavour, 56
Frank Lloyd Wright (1867 – 1959), 99
fresh herbs, 58, 59
frogs, 18, 33, 71, 73, 75, 77, 81, 84
Frogs, 85
frost, 15, 25, 27, 29, 42, 49
fruit cages, 40
fruit desserts, preserves or served in cooked sauces, 40
Fruit trees, 42
fuchsias, 29, 34
fundamental elements, 72

G

garden centres, 14, 28, 32, 36, 37, 57, 84, 86, 95
Garden ornaments, 19
garden waste, 70, 71, 72, 95
garlic, 51, 60, 74
Geraniums, 29, 90
gin, 42
Golden Bamboo, 24
Golden King holly, 24
golden yellow marsh marigold, 85

gooseberries, 39

Gooseberries, 40

green lacewings, 66

Greenfly, 71

greenfly and blackfly, 33

greenhouse, 49, 50

greenhouse gasses, 64

Gritty sand or crushed egg shells, 71

grow bags, 48, 49

growing area, 13, 45

Growing vegetables, 47, 52

growing vertically, 14

H

hanging baskets, 27, 34, 39, 49

harvest mice, 77

harvesting, 21, 35, 50, 58

healing properties, 11

health and wellbeing, 45, 55

health food shops, 54

heart disease, cancer, and diabetes, 45

hedgehogs, 70, 71, 72, 75, 81

hellebore, 65

herbs, 11, 21, 50, 54, 55, 56, 57, 58, 59, 60, 61, 94

Herbs in pots, 18

heuchera [Sugar Plum], 19

Hippocrates (c.460-370 B.C.), 55

honeysuckle, 65, 75, 90

Honeysuckle, 29

horseradish, 60

hosta, 33

hyacinth, 25

hyacinths, 26, 27, 35, 93

Hydrangeas, 34

I

Insects, 70

Iris [Iris unguicularis], 24

irises, 18

iron, 51

J

Japan, 44

Japanese quince [Chaenomeles japonica], 25

jasmine, 26, 37, 91

L

Lady Beetles, 33

ladybird beetles [a Coccinellidae beetle], 70

ladybirds beetles, 66

Lavender, 30, 89

lavender bags, 30, 58

lemon balm, 60, 65, 93

lemon balm [Melissa officinalis], 60

lemon tree, 18, 35

lily of the valley, 26, 57

liquid fertilisers, 49

Loam, 93

lobelia, 86

low maintenance designs, 13

M

Magnolia

    Magnolia Stellata, 20, 27

Magnolia Grandiflora, 20

maple, 35

marsh marigolds, 18, 28

mayflies, 85

mealybugs, 66

medicinal properties of plants and herbs, 54

meditation, 11

Michaelmas daisies, 35

mindfulness, 46, 59, 68, 99

mint, 18, 51, 57, 58, 60, 74, 86

moles, 77

Monet, 86

moths, 66, 72

mulch and compost, 35

mulches, 42, 71, 95

muntjac deer, 77

N

narcissus, 25

Narcissus, 90

nasturtium, 65

Nasturtiums, 31

Nematodes, 33

nigella, 31

nutrition, 49

O

old tales, 41

oleander, 18

olive tree, 18

oregano, 60

Organic pest control, 66

organic soil, 49

Ornamental grasses, 34

P

pak choi, 48

parasites, 66

parasitic wasps, 66

parsley, 18, 58, 60

peach tree, 18

peat-free composts, 71

penstemons, 34

peppermint, 60

Peppers, 47

Perennial herbs, 58

pests, 32, 39, 48, 67, 78

pests and diseases, 32

petunias, 28, 90

Picking fruit, 39

pigeons, 69

Plums, 44

polecats, 77

pollination, 16, 40

pollinators, 66, 75

pond skaters, 85

poppies, 31, 57, 62, 91, 94

potassium, 51

Potatoes, 50

predators, 66, 73, 84

Primroses, 25

Prunes (dried plums), 44

pruning, 41

purple, yellow or white irises, 86

pussy willow [Salix caprea], 25

pyracantha, 36, 74

Q

Queen Victoria, 44

quince, 25, 75

R

radishes, 48

Radishes, 50

raised beds, 13

Raised beds, 47

raspberries, 39, 40

rat, 69, 77

recycling food waste, 71

red leaved lettuces, 47

red poppy, 89

red rose, 20

redcurrants, 42

reduce the risk of heart disease, 40

regular watering, 49, 57

Renoir, 62

rhododendrons, 27

Rhubarb, 44

ripening, 40

roe, 77

rose hips, 35, 36

rosehips, 20

rosemary, 18, 58, 60

roses

    climbing roses, shrub roses, rambling roses and bush roses, 19, 24, 29, 31, 88, 89, 94

rudbeckia, 34, 90

runner beans, 47

S

safety, 14, 79

sage, 18, 60, 90, 93

Sandy soil, 94

scientific research, 54

sedums, 65

seeds, 15, 24, 34, 49, 52, 63, 65, 70

Self-pollinators, 43

sensory stimulus, 68

Sloe berries, 41

slugs, 33, 48, 66, 70, 75

snails, 33, 48, 70, 83

snowdrop, 90

snowdrops, 23

Snowdrops, 26

soil groups, 93

Solar power, 80

solitary bees, 66, 72

song thrushes, 71

sparrows, 71, 73

spiders, 66, 72

Spinach, 51

spiritual meaning, 67

Spring, 49, 67

spring onions, 50

Sprouts, 51

squashes, 48

squirrel, 69, 73

stag beetles, 71

staking, 25, 29, 49, 52, 96

stepping stones, 61

stoats, 77

storage and equipment, 14

strawberries, 39, 40, 45

sunflowers, 34, 93

sunspot, 49

sustaining the environment, 15

sweet cicely, 60

sweet peas, 32

Swiss chard, 47

T

tarragon, 60

Terry Irwin, 78

The Chelsea Physic Garden, 55

the Romans, 44

Therapeutic gardening, 98

thyme, 18, 58, 60, 61, 74

toads, 71, 73, 75, 77, 85

tomatoes, 48, 49, 50

tombs in Thebes, 44

trough, 20, 28, 47

U

UK peat bogs, 71

un-ripened fruits, 50

V

veganism, 47

vegetable bed, 49

vegetable gardening, 46

vegetarianism, 47

viburnum, 36

viburnums, 26

Victoria plum, 44

viper's bugloss, 65

Vitamin A, 51

vitamin C, 41, 50

vitamin C and K, 41

vitamin C, vitamin A, manganese, 41

vitamins and minerals, 47, 49, 51

W

water beetles, 85

Water lilies, 18, 86

water sounds, 80

watering in dry spells, 41

weasels, 77

weather, 15, 25, 29, 48, 84

white marguerites, 34

whiteflies, 66

whitefly, 66

wild flower garden, 62, 63

wildflower garden, 62, 64, 65, 68

Wildlife, 69, 72

wildlife pond, 79, 81, 85, 86

William Wordsworth, 96

window boxes, 48, 57, 72

winds, 48

winter heathers, 25

Winter pansies, 35

wisteria, 27

witch hazel, 23

Y

yarrow, 65

Z

zinnia, 65

www.ingramcontent.com/pod-product-compliance
Lightning Source LLC
Chambersburg PA
CBHW052158110526
44591CB00012B/1991